The 5 senses

in writing

Words Touch, Hear, See,

Smell and Taste

Copyright

Sensory techniques in texts are used to awaken the emotions and senses of the reader, making the message more vivid and impactful.

Some of the most common sensory techniques in copywriting include:

Visual: Using words that describe vivid images and scenes, such as colors, shapes, and scenery, can help create a mental picture in the reader's mind.

Tactile: Describe how things in the scene feel to the touch, such as the texture of a brick wall, the smoothness of grass, or the roughness of a stone.

Auditory: Words and phrases that describe sounds and music can help create a sensory and engaging environment for the reader.

olfactory: Using words that describe smells can evoke memories and emotions in the reader, creating an emotional connection with the message.

Gustatory: Describing flavors and textures can help create a sensory image in the reader's mind, awakening their emotions and senses.

To use these techniques in your texts, it is important to know the target audience well and understand what their main needs, desires and emotions are.

From this, it is possible to create messages thatconnect emotionally with the reader, awakening their senses and generating engagement.

Some tips for utilizing sensory techniques include:

Use descriptive words and phrases that evoke images, sounds, smells and tastes;

Create an engaging sensory atmosphere that awakens the reader's emotions and senses;

Use stories and examples to illustrate the benefits of the product or service more vividly and emotionally;

Connect the message with the needs and desires of the target audience, creating an emotional connection with the message.

In summary, sensory techniques in copywriting are a powerful way to create engaging and impactful messages that awaken the reader's emotions and senses.

A brief introduction:

When it comes to creating messages that are truly effective, it's important to keep in mind that human beings are sensory creatures. That is, we connect with the world around us through our five senses: sight, hearing, touch, smell and taste. And it is precisely this sensory connection that can make your texts even more persuasive and engaging.

By incorporating these sensory elements into your copywriting, you can create a richer and more engaging experience for the reader, making them feel more connected to the product or service being promoted.

VISION

You know that feeling of "seeing" the story being told? This is sensory vision in action, and it's one of the most powerful tools you can use to grab the reader's attention and convince them to take a specific action.

So, how to awaken the sensory vision in your texts? The answer is simple: use words that create vivid and interesting mental images in the reader's mind. Think about how you can visually describe the product or service you are promoting, and use phrases that spark the reader's imagination. For example, if you're selling a cooking course, you might describe how the vibrant colors of ingredients mix together in a hot pan, creating enticing aromas and making your mouth water.

Another tip is to use metaphors and comparisons that evoke mental images. For example, if you're selling a beauty product, you might say it makes the skin feel "like a rose petal that's soft to the touch." This creates a visual image in the reader's mind and helps convey the idea that the product is smooth and delicate.

We are naturally visual and vision is often the most powerful sense in engaging and persuading us.

There are several techniques that can be used to create images in the reader's head through words. Some of them include:

Detailed description: By describing an object, environment or situation in minute detail, the reader can better visualize what is being described.

Use of descriptive adjectives: By choosing specific and descriptive adjectives, it is possible to convey additional information about an object or situation, making the image clearer and more detailed.

Comparison and metaphor: By comparing an object or situation with something more familiar to the reader, it is possible to create a more vivid and understandable mental image.

Use of figurative language: The use of figurative language, such as symbolism, metaphors and comparisons, can help convey ideas in a more visual and impactful way.

Focus on sensations and emotions: By describing the sensations and emotions that a person might experience in a given situation, it is possible to create a more vivid and immersive image in the reader's mind.

By using these techniques, it is possible to create images in the reader's head that transport him to the story or situation described, making the reading more engaging and persuasive.

To stimulate your reader's sensory vision, you can use words that visually describe the objects, people, places or situations you are describing. Some examples of words that can help create a vivid image in the reader's mind are:

Bright

Colorful

Vibrant

Radiant

Gorgeous

sparkling

glittering

Light

Vivacious

Attractive

Charming

stunning

Fascinating

Splendid

Wonderful

In addition, it is important to use adjectives that express

visual sensations, such as:

Suave

Rough

granulated

rough

Delicate

Dirty

seeds

Slippery

Acid

Crunchy

Frozen

Soft

Wet

Translucent

Opaque

By using these words, you can help the reader to imagine the scenes you are describing more vividly and immersively.

The term "imagine" is a word that activates the reader's imagination, allowing them to create a mental picture of what is being described. This is because imagination is a complex cognitive skill that involves multiple areas of the brain, including the visual region.

When the word "imagine" is used in a descriptive context, it stimulates neural activity in these areas, allowing the reader to create a visual representation in their mind. Furthermore, the word "imagine" also suggests an invitation for the reader to actively participate in the construction of the text's meaning, making it more engaging and persuasive.

TOUCH

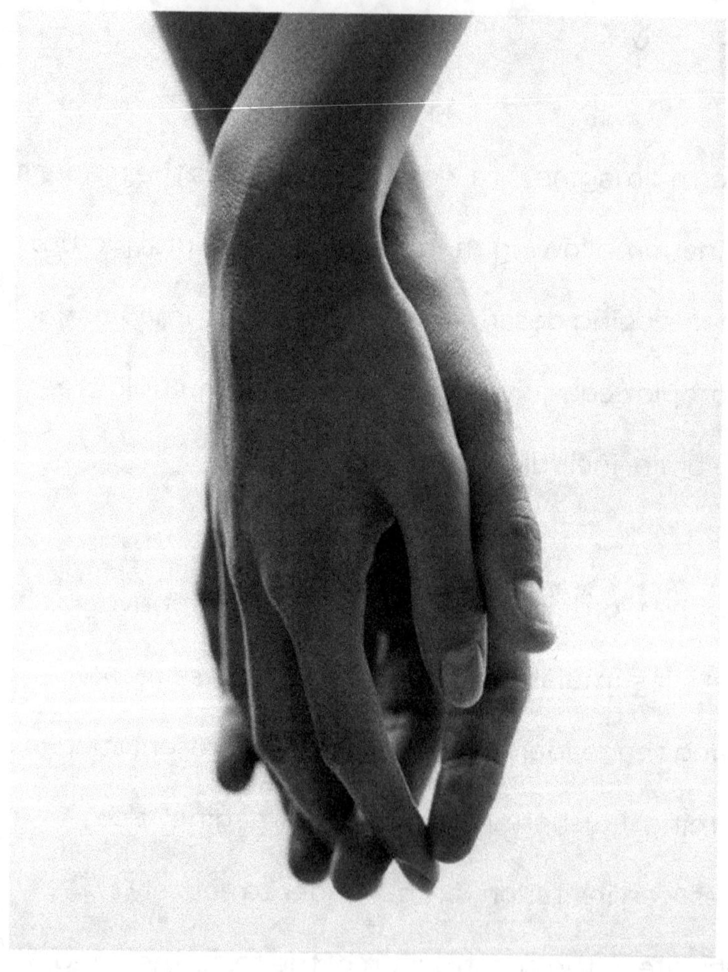

Touch is one of the most primitive and fundamental senses of human beings, being responsible for establishing immediate emotional connections with the world around them.

By using words that describe tactile sensations in your texts, it is possible to evoke memories and emotions in the reader, creating a powerful emotional connection with the message being conveyed.

It is as if the reader could feel the textures, temperatures and even the vibrations that are being described, generating a complete and unique sensory experience.

The tactile sense is often overlooked in the tech world.

When selling a computer mouse, it's easy to focus on aspects like speed, design and functionality, but neglecting touch can be a crucial mistake.

Mouse texture may seem like an insignificant detail, but it is a feature that can make all the difference in the user experience. When the user touches the mouse, the texture can influence the grip and the feeling of control, making the user experience more pleasant and intuitive. In addition, texture can evoke feelings of luxury and quality, which can be a deciding factor when choosing a product. That's why it's important to highlight the texture of the mouse when promoting it, so consumers know they're buying a product that's not only fast and beautiful, but is also pleasant to use and touch.

Some words that can be used to create the feeling of
tact in the reader are:

velvety,

rough,

soft,

suave,

rough,

textured,

seeds,

silky,

furry,

plush,

cozy,

cold,

warm,

damp,

dry,

clingy,

clingy,

firm,

denso,

thick,

light,

delicate,

rough,

granulated,

prickly,

between others.

These words can be used in detailed descriptions of

objects, fabrics, foods and other elements that can

create a tactile sensation in the reader's mind.

See other examples, now within sentences:

Feel the softness of our peach skin with our personal care products.

Experience the velvety texture of this melt-in-your-mouth chocolate cake.

Glide your fingers over the smooth, sleek surface of this cutting-edge cell phone.

Feel the softness of this high quality Egyptian cotton fabric against your skin.

Feel the crunchy texture of our irresistible fries in your mouth.

Feel the softness of this linen sheet that caresses your skin.

Experience the soft, supple feel of our real leather shoes.

Feel the delicacy of the aroma of our scented candles that spread throughout the environment.

Glide your fingers over the polished finish of this sports car that glides smoothly down the road.

In conclusion, the use of words that describe touch can be a powerful tool for creating an emotional connection with the reader, evoking memories and emotions. By using this technique in persuasive texts, it is possible to create a complete sensory experience for the reader, which can be a differential when transmitting a message or selling a product.

Therefore, it is important to remember that touch is an

often overlooked sense in writing, but one that can be

used effectively to create engaging and captivating

texts.

Hearing is a powerful sense that can help create a rich and engaging sensory experience for the reader.

Using words and phrases that describe sounds and music can help create this environment. When you describe the sound of a wave crashing on a beach, the chirping of birds, or the sound of an orchestra tuning up its instruments, the reader can imagine these sounds in their mind.

Also, music can be used as a tool to create a specific emotional environment. When the character is going through a sad time, sad music can be played in the background to intensify the emotion. When there is an action scene, upbeat music can be played to create a sense of urgency and excitement.

Using listening to create an engaging sensory environment can help the reader feel more connected to the story. That's why it's important to carefully choose words and phrases that describe sounds and music and use them strategically to create the desired atmosphere.

So if you want to take the reader on a complete sensory journey, don't forget to use words and phrases that describe sounds and music. This will help create a richer, more engaging and emotionally powerful reading experience.

To stimulate your reader's sense of hearing, you can use words and phrases that describe sounds and noises, such as:

thunderous

Delicate

Harmonious

strident

Whispering

Deafening

Melodious

sparkling

Discordant

Strange

Ecoante

beats

breath

Resonant

popping

You can use phrases that emphasize the auditory experience of the character or the environment, such as:

The sound resounded through the halls

The noise echoed in the void

The melody enveloped my ears

Drums pounded in my ears

The hiss of static cut my ears

The sound of approaching footsteps made me tense.

Birdsong echoed through the forest.

The sound of the waves soothed me

The silence was deafening

By using these words and phrases, you can help create a rich and engaging sensory environment for the reader, making them feel part of the story and emotionally involved with the characters and situations described.

Hearing can be used at different times in your texts to create a sensory connection with the reader and make reading more engaging. Some examples of times when it is interesting to use audition are:

Environment descriptions: using words that describe sounds of an environment can help the reader to imagine the scene and feel present in that space.

Storytelling: By describing the sounds characters hear in a story, the reader can feel more immersed in the plot and identify with the characters.

Advertising: by using jingles or memorable sounds in advertising campaigns, it is possible to create positive associations with the brand in the consumer's mind.

Procedural Instructions: By describing the sounds that accompany the performance of a procedure, the reader can feel more confident when performing it.

Movie theaters use hearing to create tension in their spectators through various techniques, such as: gradual increase in the volume of the soundtrack, sudden and unexpected sounds, abrupt silences, among others. These techniques are capable of activating the viewer's sympathetic nervous system, increasing their heart rate, breathing and sense of alertness.

Furthermore, careful choice of soundtrack can convey specific emotions and create an emotional connection between the viewer and the film, further increasing their involvement with the plot.

Instagram posts themselves tend to convert more with music in the background due to a number of factors.

First and foremost, music is a form of auditory stimulation that can help grab the viewer's attention and make content more engaging and engaging. Furthermore, careful choice of music can convey specific emotions and create an emotional connection between the viewer and the posted content, increasing the likelihood of engagement and sharing.

Another important factor is the possibility of using popular songs that are already known by the public, which can generate an immediate identification and a feeling of familiarity. As a result, songs can help set the tone and style of the content, reinforcing the identity of the brand or creator of the content.

In summary, listening can be used at various times in your texts to create an emotional connection with the reader and make reading more engaging and memorable.

OLFACTORY

When we remember something, we usually associate that memory with a specific smell. This is why the use of words that describe smells can be so powerful in writing. These words can evoke memories and emotions in the reader, creating an emotional connection with the message.

By describing a scent, you can transport the reader to a specific place and help them feel immersed in the story. For example, by describing the smell of a bakery on a sunny morning, you can help the reader feel like they're there. Or by describing the smell of a campfire on a cold night, you can help the reader feel the warmth and coziness of the scene.

In addition, smells can be used to create a specific emotional environment. A pleasant scent can evoke feelings of joy and happiness, while an unpleasant smell can evoke feelings of disgust and disgust. By using words that describe smells, you can help create a rich and engaging sensory experience for the reader, evoking emotions and sensations they may not have experienced before.

So if you want to create a strong emotional connection with the reader, don't forget to use words that describe smells. These words can help evoke memories and emotions in the reader, creating a richer and more engaging reading experience.

Use words and phrases that describe smells and aromas, such as:

Aromatic

sweetened

Sour

woody

Fresco

Spicy

vinegary

Citric

Floral

malodorous

Bread

Metallic

Musky

Fragrant

Rotten

Spicy

Pungent

Dirty

sweetened

Suave

But you can also use phrases that emphasize the olfactory experience of the character or the environment, such as:

The smell of freshly baked bread

The sweet scent of roses

The woody scent of the forest

The smell of freshly cut grass

The aroma of fresh, hot coffee

The smell of smoke from a burning fireplace

The aroma of spices on a hot plate

The smell of fresh fish at the market

The scent of wildflowers in spring

The smell of rain in the air

By using these words and phrases, you can help create a rich and engaging sensory environment for the reader, making them feel part of the story and emotionally involved with the characters and situations described.

PALATE

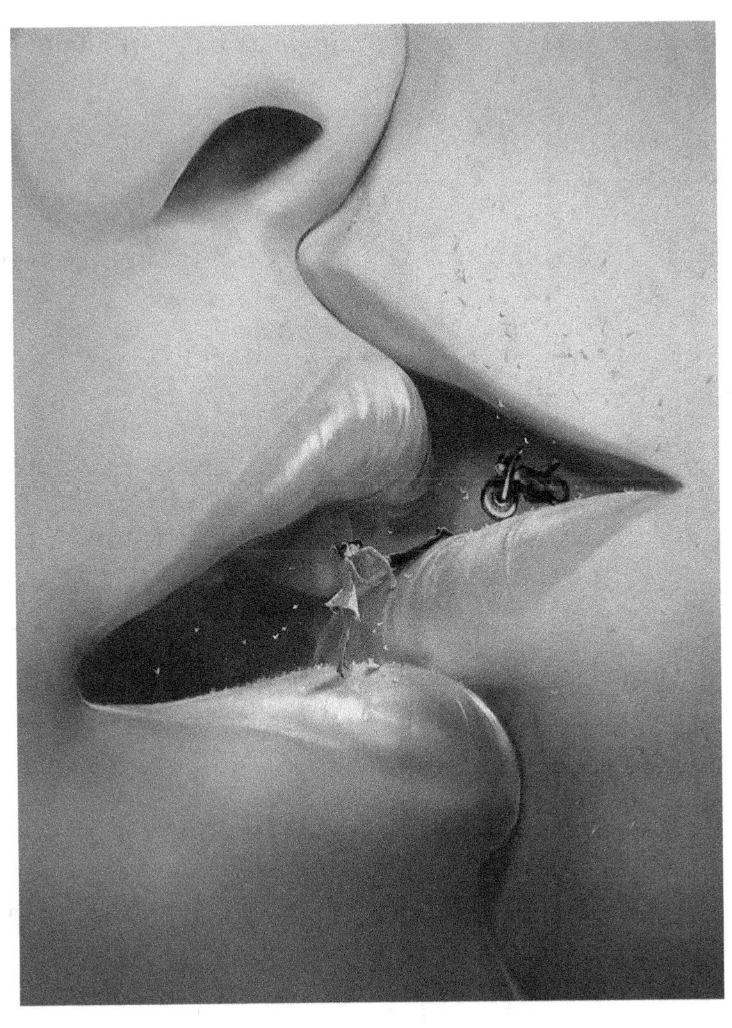

The choice of words and phrases used to describe flavors and textures can make all the difference in how the message is received by the public.

Words like "creamy", "crunchy", "sour", "sweet", "bitter" and "salty" can help create a vivid and realistic image in the reader's mind, stimulating their taste buds and imagination.

In addition, it is important to remember that the choice of words must also be in accordance with the target audience and the message you want to convey. It is possible to use more technical and specific words for a more specialized audience, for example, or simpler and familiar words for a broader audience.

By using the technique of describing flavors and textures, it is possible to create a richer and more engaging sensorial experience for the reader, making him feel part of the story and emotionally connected with the transmitted message.

If you want to stimulate the sense of taste in the reader, it is important to use words and phrases that describe the flavors, textures and sensations that a food can provoke. Some words that can be used are:

Sweet: sugary, honeyed, caramelised, smooth, soft, melty, creamy, velvety;

Salted: medium salted, peppered, brine, smoked, crispy, hard, salted just right;

Sour: acidic, citric, fresh, sour, bitter, astringent;

Bitter: strong, dense, full-bodied, intense, deep, persistent;

Picante: fiery, spicy, strong, spicy, exciting, intense;

Others: smooth, crunchy, soft, dry, moist, crusty, stringy, silky, crunchy.

By using these and similar words, it is possible to awaken taste sensations in the reader, creating an engaging and sensorial experience.

But remember that the choice of words must be in tune with the message and the target audience, creating an authentic and pleasant taste experience. Some example sentences include:

Dessert was a creamy, delicate ice cream with a smooth vanilla flavor and crunchy pieces of caramelized almonds.

The main course was a juicy, tender filet with a sauce rich in flavors and textures that enveloped the tongue.

The fresh, crunchy salad was a mix of vibrant flavors and colors, with a spicy kick of pepper and a sweet and sour dressing that brought out the flavors of the ingredients.

The coffee had a rich, inviting aroma, with a strong, lingering aftertaste that warmed the mouth.

The full-bodied red wine had a deep, complex flavor, with hints of dark fruit and a hint of oak that accentuated the flavor.

The carrot cake was soft and moist, with a fluffy texture and a sweet, delicate flavor that melted in your mouth.

By using words that awaken taste sensations, for example, it is possible to create an emotional bond with the advertised product or service, increasing the chances of conversion. Therefore, it is important to invest in techniques that stimulate the reader's senses, creating an emotional and sensorial connection with the transmitted message.

When a person thinks of something that is tasty or that arouses their taste buds, the brain can send signals to the autonomic nervous system, which is responsible for controlling involuntary bodily functions, including saliva production. These signals can stimulate the salivary glands, which begin to secrete saliva into the mouth in preparation for eating.

This is because the brain associates the thought of tasty food with the actual experience of eating and consequently triggers a physiological response in the body. This response is a way to prepare the body for food intake and ensure that the digestion process takes place properly.

In addition, saliva has the function of lubricating the mouth and helping with chewing and swallowing food. Therefore, saliva production in response to a tasty thought can be seen as a way of preparing the body for food intake and ensuring that the digestion process

takes place efficiently.

The 5 senses used for good

and the 5 senses used for evil

It is possible to use the 5 sensory senses both to highlight the advantages of your product or service and to disqualify your competitors.

By exploring the sensory senses, you can create an emotional connection with your target audience, making them feel attracted to your product or service.

On the other hand, by highlighting the lack of quality of your competitors' products or services in terms of sensory experience, you can undermine your potential customers' trust in your competitors and, consequently, increase the chance that they will choose your product or service.

I'll show you this in practical examples.

Positive example:

Imagine yourself sitting in a dining chair that is a true sensory experience. The smooth texture of the velvet upholstery is a real treat for your hands, while the absolute silence of the structure ensures that you can enjoy pleasant conversation and the company of your loved ones. The high, padded backrest provides comfortable support for your spine, allowing you to fully relax while enjoying a delicious meal. In addition, the dining chair's sophisticated and elegant design is a real masterpiece, which adds a touch of glamor and elegance to your home.

Negative example:

Now imagine yourself in a dining chair that is anything but sensory. The squeaky noise of the structure as you move around can make you uncomfortable and even interrupt your conversation. The hard, uncomfortable seat makes you want to get up as quickly as possible, making eating a real agony. Furthermore, the design of the chair is drab and bland, adding little to no aesthetic value to your home. This chair is a real disappointment to your senses and a waste of money.

However, it is important to remember that ethics and honesty are fundamental in any marketing strategy, and that false claims and exaggerations must be avoided in order not to damage the credibility of your brand.

A PREDOMINANT CHOICE

Choosing which sensory sense to use in a product or service can be a difficult task, but it is essential for the public to connect emotionally with what is being offered.

Each sense can evoke different emotions and sensations, so it is important to think carefully about the one that most predominates in the experience offered.

It is important to point out that the choice should not be made just by personal preference, but thinking about the benefits that the product or service offers and how they can be communicated more effectively through a specific sensory sense.

For example, if the product is a perfume, the choice of the sense of smell is obvious, as it is through smell that the fragrance is experienced.

Likewise, if the product is a meal, the sense of taste should be chosen to highlight the flavor characteristics.

The problem is that everyone does it.

My suggestion is...

Choose a predominant sense that best matches the product and then choose others to create more connection with your audience.

When choosing a sensory sense to predominate, it is also important to think about the benefits it brings. For example, when using vision on a product, it is possible to highlight its beauty or attractive aesthetics. Touch can evoke a sense of comfort or warmth.

In summary, the choice of sensory sense must be strategic and made thinking about the benefits it brings to the consumer's experience. When chosen wisely, it can be a powerful tool for creating an emotional connection and increasing the effectiveness of the communicated message.

The framework for the 5 senses

Here is a suggested chronological order for using the 5 senses in the same text with persuasion techniques:

Start with the vision: Use words that describe a vivid scene that the reader can imagine. It could be a lush landscape or an exciting scene that captures the reader's attention.

Then add touch: Describe how things in the scene feel to the touch, such as the texture of a brick wall, the smoothness of grass, or the roughness of a stone.

Add smell: Describe smells in the scene, such as the smell of fresh grass, the scent of fragrant flowers, or the salty smell of the ocean.

Add taste: Describe flavors the reader can sense in the scene, such as the salty taste of sea air or the sweet taste of fresh fruit.

Finally, add hearing: Describe sounds in the scene, such as birdsong, the sound of waves, or music in the background.

By using these techniques, it is possible to create an emotional and sensory connection with the reader, making them feel more involved and engaged with the content. However, it is important to remember that these techniques should be used in a way that is subtle and relevant to the subject being addressed, in order to avoid appearing over the top or forced.

CONCLUSION

Each sense is responsible for capturing a type of stimulus from the environment and sending this information to the brain so that it can be interpreted and processed. Understanding the five senses is essential to understanding how humans and other animals interact with their environment and how language can be used to evoke different sensations in readers.

It is possible to use the 5 senses in any product or service, regardless of its nature. From food to financial services, passing through electronics and clothing, all items have the potential to be explored through the senses. When describing the characteristics of a product or service, it is possible to use words that evoke gustatory, olfactory, tactile, visual and sound sensations.

This creates a complete sensory experience for the

consumer, who can feel more connected and

emotionally involved with what they are buying. Using

the 5 senses in your texts can be an effective way to

differentiate your product or service from the

competition and to generate a stronger connection with

your customers.

BONUS

Activating the sixth sense

Now that we've explored techniques for using the five senses in texts, it's time to address the sixth sense.

Although there is no clear and scientific definition of the sixth sense, it is often associated with intuition or extrasensory perception. However, we can think of activating a "sixth sense" in the reader as a way of creating a sense of surprise or expectation in the text, something that may surprise or challenge the reader's expectations.

One way to activate the reader's "sixth sense" is through the use of narrative techniques that create tension, suspense or mystery in the text, leaving the reader curious and intrigued about what will happen next. This can be done through elements such as cryptic dialogues, mysterious characters or unexpected events.

Furthermore, the use of figurative or symbolic language can help to create a sense of depth or deeper meaning in the text, something that can stimulate the reader's imagination and lead him to reflect on the text's message in a deeper way.

In summary, to activate a "sixth sense" in the reader, it is important to create a sense of anticipation, mystery or deeper meaning in the text, through the use of narrative techniques and figurative language.

Activating the senses in words is a highly effective strategy to win over any reader and generate an explosion of sales.

It is as if we are playing with an unfair advantage, as it is almost cowardly to arouse the reader's emotions and senses so powerfully.

After all, when we use rich and detailed sensory descriptions, we transport the reader into the story and make him feel, smell, hear, see and even taste the narrated experiences.

This sensorial immersion is capable of creating a strong emotional connection between the reader and the story, considerably increasing the chances of sales and loyalty.

Therefore, if you want to create engaging and highly persuasive texts, do not hesitate to explore all the senses and provide a complete experience for whoever is on the other side of the words.

Who is Matheus Martins Soares?

Matheus is an Ex-Military / Presidential Agent, graduated in Marketing since 2018 and specialist in copywriting. He has written for more than 27 different niches, showing his ability to adapt to different topics and audiences. Throughout his career, he has worked in large companies, such as the largest business magazine in the country and the largest marketing consultancy in Brazil. Contributed to the success of important campaigns, generating + 30mm in sales for its customers. Published over 100 books on Amazon and gained readers in over 10 different countries. An expert in StoryTelling and UX Writing, he also works behind the scenes as a GhostWriter, giving voice to other people's ideas and stories. His method is capable of writing a book in less than 24 hours.

With a strategic vision and knowledge in marketing, he helps companies, authors and literary projects to achieve success. He found himself in the world of marketing, writing and human behavior, his ability to adapt to different challenges is a differential that makes him stand out in his field.